God and the Indian

Also by Drew Hayden Taylor

PLAYS

alterNatives*
The Baby Blues*
The Berlin Blues*
The Bootlegger Blues
The Boy in the Treehouse / Girl Who Loved Her Horses*
The Buz'Gem Blues*
Dead White Writer on the Floor*
400 Kilometres*
In a World Created by a Drunken God*
Only Drunks and Children Tell the Truth*
Someday
Toronto at Dreamer's Rock / Education Is Our Right

FICTION

Fearless Warriors*
Motorcycles and Sweetgrass
The Night Wanderer

NON-FICTION

Me Funny
Me Sexy
NEWS: Postcards from the Four Directions*

* Available from Talonbooks

God
and
the
Indian

———— a play ————

DREW HAYDEN TAYLOR

Talonbooks

Talonbooks
278 East First Avenue, Vancouver, British Columbia, Canada V5T 1A6
www.talonbooks.com

First printing: 2014

Typeset in Sabon
Printed and bound in Canada on 100% post-consumer recycled paper

Interior and cover design by Typesmith
Cover illustration by Chloë Filson

Talonbooks gratefully acknowledges the financial support of the Canada Council for the Arts, the Government of Canada through the Canada Book Fund, and the Province of British Columbia through the British Columbia Arts Council and the Book Publishing Tax Credit.

Library and Archives Canada Cataloguing in Publication

Taylor, Drew Hayden, 1962–, author
God and the Indian / Drew Hayden Taylor.

A play.
Issued in print and electronic formats.
ISBN 978-0-88922-844-3 (PBK.).—ISBN 978-0-88922-845-0 (EPUB)

        I. Title.

PS8589.A885G63 2014   C812'.54   C2014-900163-0
                                           C2014-900164-9

To the lovely Janine,
without whose patience and support
I could not have written these words

Preface

Those familiar with my work will agree that, for better or worse, *God and the Indian* is a departure for me. Let me tell you how the play came to be, from the beginning.

I had never really intended to write a play about the residential school issue. It seemed everybody and their grandmother was pulling their own page out of that book and I didn't want to be part of that trend, having never been to such a school. The voices of many other authors, who personally experienced that tragic period, were also, I thought, more authentic than my own. My voice is that of the humorist; I am known primarily for – but not limited to – a lighthearted and satirical take on the Native experience. Cultural genocide and institutionalized sexual abuse do not lend themselves to humour very well. Nor should they.

One spring day I was chatting with the artistic director of a Native theatre company where I was the new writer-in-residence ("new" being a somewhat inaccurate term to describe me, as I had served as the writer-in-residence for this company twenty years earlier). During an initial meeting, the AD stated unequivocally her aims for my residency. "Drew, I don't want you to write something fun and enjoyable," she said. "I want you to write something bleak and depressing."

Maybe I'm exaggerating. In truth, she said something closer to, "I know you can be funny. I want to see you be serious," forgetting that the year before I had been shortlisted for the Governor General's Award for *In a World Created by a Drunken God*, a serious drama and one of my most successful works to date. I remember being surprised by this request. Very rarely, other than in a direct commission, have I been told specifically what I can and cannot write. I already had a whole play planned out in my head, waiting to spring forth and fill the seats of that theatre. I can't help but wonder if this AD has ever told any of her more serious and sombre playwrights, "Okay, I know you can be serious. But I want to see if you can be funny." Probably not.

I decided to take the bit in my teeth and accept the challenge. In order to please the boss, I tried to think of the most depressing and painful thing happening in the Native community that I could write about. Thus the idea for *God and the Indian* was born.

I realize this may sound like a frivolous or superficial approach to the issue, but in the end it wasn't. Sincerely motivated to write this story honourably and with respect, I threw myself into it. If I screwed up, if I was flippant, if I was disrespectful, I would definitely hear about it. And rightly so. At the time of my residency with the theatre, the Truth and Reconciliation Commission hearings were being held across the country and, let's face it, you cannot be Native in Canada without knowing someone who was personally affected by the residential school system. Research was easy. Coming up with the story was easy. Being honest and humble in telling this story was more challenging – but essential. I began to write.

Some months later, I submitted the first draft. It was a two-act play, admittedly with some dark humour in it, about a man trying to find closure. Either by accident or by act of God, he sees a man from his past – a man who was an Anglican minister at the residential school he attended decades earlier and who had abused him. He follows the minister to his office and demands accountability.

One of the most surprising things I learned in my research is that many residential school survivors aren't looking for vengeance or retribution. They just want to be heard. They just want to be believed. And that's what Johnny, my central character, wants from the now assistant bishop. Johnny wants to hear the man acknowledge and own up to his actions. Who wouldn't?

A week or so later, I heard back from the AD. She thought I should cut my full-length play to one act. Not really agreeing with her, but knowing that she who signs the cheques is seldom wrong, I gutted my play. That is to say, I ripped twenty or thirty pages from the middle of the script, without understanding why, and resubmitted it. Strangely, another week or two went by before I heard back from the theatre company. Now they were not interested in my serious play and wished me good luck submitting it elsewhere.

Feeling a little angry and petulant after this incident, I set *God and the Indian* aside and forgot about it. Almost completely. I tucked it away in some obscure file on my computer and in my mind, concentrating instead on other stories and tales that were waiting to be written, with hopefully a lot less baggage. The play stayed buried for several years until I ran into one of the former board members of the theatre company. He asked whatever happened to that play about residential school. Apparently he liked what I had written and was puzzled why it had never gone any further. It took me a moment to remember what play he was talking about.

Remembering its resonance, I subsequently went home, dug it out (the two-act version), reread it, and recognized its definite possibilities. One opinion is not the only opinion. So, getting a second breath of interest, I decided to submit it to other theatre companies that were interested in my work. That's where Donna Spencer at Vancouver's Firehall Arts Centre comes into the picture. She read it and liked it, and a new dialogue between AD and playwright began.

But there was one minor problem. No older male First Nations actors were available for the role of Johnny, the residential school survivor. But miraculously, for some reason unknown to me, the magnificent Tantoo Cardinal had heard about the play and expressed interest in playing the role of Johnny. Now, I am sure you realize the difficulty inherent in that possibility.

Donna asked how determined I was that the character of Johnny be male. The physical, emotional, and sexual mistreatment in those schools favoured neither male nor female students, and the repercussions of that abuse has permeated generations of Natives, regardless of gender. So, intrigued, I decided to explore the concept of a female Johnny. The more I thought about it and rewrote the script, the more the female Johnny came into focus and the more excited I became. Tantoo, as Johnny, opened up unexplored character possibilities and I found myself writing new and exciting material that I had not even considered during *God and the Indian*'s first iterations.

To make a long story slightly shorter, after some rewrites the play was produced in spring 2013 at the Firehall Arts Centre. It was marvellously envisioned and directed by Renae Morriseau, staring Tantoo and Michael Kopsa. The final play script you now hold in your hands. In these pages I ask some questions, but answer only a few of them; others I leave up to you to decide.

This is an angry play. This is a healing play. This play is many things. I only hope I have done the topic and the people justice.

I hope I was serious enough.

DREW HAYDEN TAYLOR
Curve Lake, Ontario
February 2014

God and the Indian was first produced on April 7, 2013, at the Firehall Arts Centre in Vancouver, British Columbia, with the following cast and creative team:

JOHNNY	Tantoo Cardinal
GEORGE	Michael Kopsa
Director	Renae Morriseau
Set and Lighting Designer	Lauchlin Johnson
Costume Designer	Alex Danard
Artistic Director	Donna Spencer
Stage Manager	Robin Richardson

CHARACTERS

Johnny: Native woman, panhandler, residential school survivor, early fifties

George: Caucasian, assistant bishop in the Anglican Church, former teacher at an Anglican residential school, mid-sixties

SETTING

The assistant bishop's office, located in an old mansion that has been converted to offices

TIME

Early 2000s

ACT ONE

*Lights up on a modest but well-appointed office
in a heritage mansion that has been converted to
offices. A large wooden desk sits in one corner. On
the wall behind it hangs a painting of Christ with
children gathered around him. An overstuffed chair,
a mini-bar, a bookshelf, and a small couch and coffee
table furnish the rest of the room.*

*It is Saturday morning. Scattered about the office
is evidence of a small party from the night before:
folding chairs leaning against one wall, wrapping
paper from presents, trays of food in various states
of consumption, and, directly in front of the door,
a large cardboard box filled with empty wine bottles.
There is silence. The door opens revealing Assistant
Bishop GEORGE LINUS KING. Looking content, he
enters, sets his Tim Hortons coffee cup on the desk,
and hangs up his coat. He is a well-dressed man of
confidence and status, and it shows.*

GEORGE

(*addressing the painting*) Good morning, my Saviour.
Another beautiful day you've given us. (*takes a sip of
coffee*) As God is my witness, I do not understand the
appeal of Tim Hortons. It's blander than a Catholic
sermon. Still, it will keep me humble (*begins making
coffee in his own coffee maker*) till I get to the good stuff.
(*looks around*) My goodness, what a mess, but I'm not
afraid to get my hands dirty. It's not exactly washing
feet, but thy will be done … (*He sniffs, noticing the smell*

from one of the trays.) Day-old sushi ... and whole-wheat crackers ... not quite five loaves of bread and two fishes ...

Waiting for the coffee to brew, GEORGE begins to clean up the office. He notices an overturned family photograph on the shelf. He picks it up and places it right side up on his desk. He smiles with satisfaction at this moment of domesticity and resumes tidying up. He places several bottles of expensive alcohol – gifts from the night before – on the desk. As he works, he begins to hum Anglican hymn 143, "Forgive them Father, for they know not what they do." He examines the bottles.

GEORGE

Vermouth. Grand Marnier. Who gives these as presents to an Anglican minister? Is that your way of telling me I'm gonna really need this for my new position? I heard you work in mysterious ways, but that could have just been a rumour.

GEORGE notices a wrapped box in the corner and picks it up. He tears away the wrapping paper to reveal a new espresso machine.

GEORGE

An espresso machine! You do answer prayers.

GEORGE continues cleaning up the room, humming to himself. Quietly, the door to his office opens. A Native woman enters. She is wearing many layers of old, torn clothing to keep out the cold, and her hair is dirty. She seems tired and worn out, and as though she's been left behind by both societies. Busy tidying, GEORGE doesn't notice her at first. Finally he turns and sees her in the doorway. He is startled.

GEORGE

HOLY MARY MOTHER OF GOD! (*gathers himself together*)

You scared me! I'm sorry, but this is a private office. You're not supposed to be in here.

The woman is silent for a moment, first taking in the room, then GEORGE, before responding.

JOHNNY

Nintoogeewaan. (I want to go home.)

GEORGE

I'm sorry. What did you say?

JOHNNY

Nintoogeewaan. (I want to go home.)

GEORGE

I'm sorry … I don't … It's okay. I think you've wandered into the wrong place. We can't help you here. But the shelter is just three blocks down. You can get warm there, and they have coffee. Food, too.

JOHNNY laughs.

GEORGE

What's so funny?

JOHNNY

"We can't help you here." Man, if you'd only known that forty years ago, you coulda saved us both a lot of trouble.

GEORGE

Ah, you speak English.

JOHNNY

Yep. You taught it to me. *A* is for "apple." *B* is for … "bullshit" or something.

GEORGE

I taught it to you?

JOHNNY

Yeah, you people. White people. Anglican people. White
Anglican people. You almost taught me too good. What
I just said is all I remember of how my parents talked.
Their language. I remember it 'cause I used to say it to
myself all the time. There at the school. So many times
when I was lying in bed, or when I was locked in the closet.
"I want to go home" – that's what it means. I could be
dead a month and still be able to say it. *Nintoogeewaan.*

GEORGE

How did you get in here, anyway? The door should be –

JOHNNY

It is. But the thing about these old buildings is they
often have old, very breakable glass somewhere around.
You'll see that somebody broke into that room where the
photocopier is, down there in the basement. You should
be more careful; you never know who or what might
crawl in here.

GEORGE

I see. And just why are you here?

JOHNNY

That's a very long story. But it's got a happy ending, 'cause
I think I already found what I was lookin' for.

GEORGE

Perhaps I should call the police.

JOHNNY

You don't have to do that. I've already been punished.

JOHNNY holds up her hand, and it's bleeding.

GEORGE

Oh my god.

JOHNNY

That old glass is kinda thin and sharp. (*looks to her hand*)
Sorta looks like one of those stig- ... things ... you know,
bleeding like Jesus did that time on the Cross.

GEORGE

I think you mean stigmata.

JOHNNY

Yeah, that's it.

GEORGE

Well, I can assure you it's not. That's just Catholic
superstition.

JOHNNY

Good. It would be very inconvenient to find out I was
a Catholic saint.

*GEORGE immediately becomes concerned with her
wound. He looks around for something suitable
to bandage her cut, but ends up using his scarf.
JOHNNY flinches, seemingly afraid of GEORGE,
but he continues to attend to her wound, being very
careful not to come in contact with her blood.*

GEORGE

Do you mind? I won't hurt you. Oh dear, that looks deep.

JOHNNY

Look at my blood. It seems so red, eh, and everything else
so ... colourless. The funny thing is, it don't really hurt. It
should hurt. I used to hurt.

JOHNNY squeezes her fist so that blood oozes out.

JOHNNY

Sometimes when I throw up, it's that colour. Funny, eh?

GEORGE cleans her cut very delicately, wary of getting any blood on himself. He grabs the nearest bottle of alcohol and prepares to pour some on the cut.

JOHNNY

What a waste.

GEORGE

Those windows are filthy. You might need to get a tetanus shot. Now this is gonna sting a bit.

JOHNNY

Go ahead. Can't feel a thing.

He douses the cut.

GEORGE

Here, keep pressure on it. That looks nasty. I'm sorry, I didn't catch your name. (*pause*) You are ...

Absent-mindedly, GEORGE wipes some blood off the arm of the couch.

JOHNNY

That's a good question. (*pause*) I don't know.

GEORGE

You don't know your name?

JOHNNY

I know who I used to be. I know who I was supposed to be. But that was a long time ago. Who I am today ... like I said, that's one good question.

GEORGE

It's actually quite a simple question. You really should have somebody look at that. It's quite deep.

JOHNNY

I'll put it on my list of things to do.

GEORGE

Well, whoever you are, the hospital is two blocks away. They'll take care of you. I can find somebody to take you over there. I'd do it myself, but I have a lot of work to do.

JOHNNY

Like maybe … the work of God?

GEORGE

Well, we *are* the Anglican Church.

JOHNNY

Yeah, I saw the sign out front. I got a question for you. Me. You don't remember me, do you?

GEORGE

You? No. I can't say that I do. What's your name?

JOHNNY

What's my name?

GEORGE

Yes, what is your name?

JOHNNY

I would tell you, but I think maybe that's too easy. You see, sometimes I don't even know. Sometimes it becomes hazy. Sometimes I'm not sure I'm seeing what I'm seeing. It gets hard.

GEORGE

Listen, it's clear you have some issues, but I am not prepared to deal with them at the moment. I'm not without sympathy. Let me pay for a cab to –

JOHNNY

Like this morning. I was on my corner. It's not my usual corner. A couple of punks took it over a while ago. They don't let me sit there anymore. They have really bad attitudes. They don't love their neighbour. Me, I blame television. So I try this new place, just a couple of blocks down the street, in front of that Tim Hortons. I figure it's as good a place as any to make some money, and a lady's gotta do something with her life or she ain't a lady. Do you know what I'm saying, sir?

GEORGE
Look, I really …

JOHNNY
So, I'd been there about an hour, gotten a couple of bucks. Or maybe it was two hours … no more than three, I'm sure. Anyway, my fingers start to go numb from the cold, 'cause I'm out there so long. So, I'm sitting there, canvassing the citizens of this city for some *disposable income* … You know, I like talking like that sometimes. Makes me feel kinda smart. I learn more big words from them social workers than I did from you. Funny, eh?

> JOHNNY *appears weak at times. She is wracked by a seizure of pain. Her voice falters.*

GEORGE
What's wrong? Are you sick?

JOHNNY
Yeah, pretty sick. Both body and soul, as my *noogoom* would say …

GEORGE
We should get you to that hospital …

JOHNNY
Oh, been there lots already. So many people complain about hospital food, but hospital food is sure better than no food. Those hospital people can't do much for me, anyways.

GEORGE
Still …

JOHNNY

No, no, I'll be okay. It goes away after a while. Where was I... Oh yeah, I was sitting there at Timmy Hortons, watching people get their coffee this morning, when I saw you. You sure walk fast.

GEORGE

You followed me from ... from the Tim Hortons?

JOHNNY

Yep. I recognized you.

GEORGE

Really, I don't think we've ever met. I'm new to the diocese.

JOHNNY

Oh, we met. Long time ago. Me, I've changed a bit since the last time you saw me. Put on about two feet and maybe forty or more pounds. All the doughnuts, I think.

JOHNNY starts to remove her outer layers of clothing.

GEORGE

Excuse me, please don't get comfortable. You can't stay here.

JOHNNY

Again, if you'd told me that forty years ago, it would have saved us both a lot of trouble. I get hot and cold flashes, which, depending where I am, don't help me a whole lot. If only I would get them hot flashes during the winter and the cold flashes during the summer, I think I'd be a much happier person. For sure. But like always, what I want makes no difference in this world. (*looks around*) This is a nice place, sir. I take it you're not a humble reverend anymore. I guess when you've taught at a residential school, there's no place to move but up.

GEORGE

How … how did you know I used to teach at –

JOHNNY

Ah, I think I got your attention now. St. David's. That's
where I know you from. Did I mention you look a lot
better now? Filled out a bit, and you sure dress better. You
got a better job, too, I see. But yeah, it's still you. Someone
can't change that much. You still stand the same and, after
all these years, your hair is still the same. What's left of it.
Yeah, I remember you, from St. David's, all that time ago.
Some stuff in my head still works, but then again, you're
a hard man to forget.

GEORGE

I think … that you need to leave.

JOHNNY

Boy, we've both come a long way, eh? Somehow, though,
I think you did a little better in life than me. I guess it helps
when you are the same race as God.

>   GEORGE *is silent*.

JOHNNY

Like I said, you're a pretty fast walker. I mean, I'm younger
then you, but, man, I had to race to keep up. Not bad
for an old man. But then again, I ain't in the best shape
myself. Still, I got hopes for the next Olympics. Thought
maybe we could catch up on old times. See how the gang is
all doing. That kind of thing. You see, I've been living on
the street so long that I'm sure my invitation to the class
reunion got lost in the mail. Remember them old days?

GEORGE

I taught there for only two years, before I was transferred.

JOHNNY

It's not how long you were somewhere; it's the memories you leave behind.

GEORGE

What did you say your name was?

JOHNNY

I didn't. That would be too easy. Remember how at school you always told us you couldn't give us the answers? That we had to find them ourselves? Now it's your turn.

GEORGE

Look, I don't know what you're up to but I don't have time for it.

JOHNNY

Really? I got nothing but time. To just remember the old days. In fact, that's my full-time job.

GEORGE

Remember the old days somewhere else!

JOHNNY is quiet, thinking.

GEORGE

Then tell me what your name is. (*pause*) Well?

JOHNNY

You can call me ...

GEORGE

Yes?

JOHNNY

Johnny. Johnny Indian.

GEORGE

What is this, a joke? What kind of name is that?

JOHNNY

It's as good as any. Better than some. Johnny Indian.
Me Johnny Indian. Like it?

GEORGE

Johnny is a man's name.

JOHNNY

It's also a white man's name. And as you can tell, I ain't
neither. That much I'm sure of. That's all just part of the
mystery of life I guess. Bummer, eh?

GEORGE

Fine. Johnny Indian. It's been a pleasure. Now
please leave.

JOHNNY

You know, a long time ago, my people had long, beautiful
Indian names that just rolled off the tongue. They sounded
like the land we came from. Colourful names. Pretty
names. Then you guys showed up and changed everything.
You decided to give us names you thought were better.
And easier. Smith. Williams. MacGregor. Scottish names,
French names, English names, and a whole bunch of
others. Names that weren't us. Names that were you.

GEORGE

You followed me here to give me a history lesson?

JOHNNY

I didn't like the name you guys gave me. It had too many
bad memories. So I decided to get a new one. Now I am
Johnny Indian. Ms. Johnny Indian. Kind of has a nice
sound to it, don't it? I'd show you my ID if I had any. I'll
answer to Johnny. Johnny Indian. Ms. Indian. Or just J.I.

GEORGE

Okay, Johnny, it's obvious you're ill, so I am going to call –

JOHNNY sees the family photograph on his desk.

JOHNNY

Hey, that your wife and kids? Good-looking family. Very
white. You should be proud. I don't have a family myself
anymore. At least I don't think so. Did I tell you things
sometimes get a bit hazy? Sometimes I forget what I tell
people. What are their names? Your family, I mean.

GEORGE

Their names are none of your business. Tell me, Johnny.
Following strangers home from Tim Hortons ... Isn't that
kind of dangerous? Or is this some kind of shakedown.

JOHNNY

No. You're not a stranger, remember? We go way back.

GEORGE

Ah yes, you know me. From St. David's.

JOHNNY

Yeah, I know you. From St. David's. You could say we
know each other in many ways. What's it called ... in
"the biblical sense." That's it, isn't it? Kinda a weird way
to describe what you used to do.

That stops GEORGE in his tracks.

GEORGE
What?

JOHNNY

I used to have a picture of my family, a thousand years
ago. Mom, Dad, my grandma, and my little brother. It
was taken a month before we were sent to the school. They
took my picture away from me, but I still have it up here.
(*indicates her head*) They can't take that away from me.
God knows they tried. I can still see my family sometimes,
when I close my eyes. My picture was in black and white,
not colour like yours. (*notices the painting*) Wow! You
know, because of you guys, I always imagined Jesus was

white. That one painting in the rectory even had him with blond hair and blue eyes. Then I found out he was one of them Jews. Now I always picture him as that *Seinfeld* guy.

GEORGE

What did you say?

JOHNNY

Seinfeld. It's a show on television. Sometimes we watch it over at the shelter –

GEORGE

About us knowing each other. Did you just accuse me of something?

JOHNNY

I don't know. Did I?

GEORGE

All right, I'm calling the authorities. They'll know how to deal with you.

JOHNNY

Not very Christian, Reverend King.

> *GEORGE has the telephone in his hand, but stops when he hears his name.*

GEORGE

You read my name on the door.

> *JOHNNY opens the door and looks at the nameplate.*

JOHNNY

Hey, there it is. And you're an assistant bishop now, to boot. Good for you. You always knew how to go after what you wanted. The residential school couldn't hold you ... unlike the rest of us. But who could forget the good Reverend George Linus King, the King of St. David's? A lot of the kids called you King David. But always remember, the higher up you are, the farther you have to fall. You taught us that. So, you just call the police. I'll wait over here. Rest my old bones.

JOHNNY picks up a bottle off the desk and squints at the label.

JOHNNY

Grand Marn … iar! What the hell is that? Go ahead, call them police. We'll all have a drink and chat. I've got a few things to tell them, too. We'll talk all morning. You know I used to drink? A lot. I know I hide it well. Ooh, Scotch. Had a boyfriend who was Scottish, long time ago. Fresh off the boat. Man, he was a looker and, when he got drunk, his accent got thicker and thicker. When he was really blasted, it suddenly turned into a completely different language. I think he called it "garlic" or something. I knew a lot of old Indian drunks would do the same. Get drunker and drunker until they only spoke Indian. Mind if I take a sniff?

GEORGE doesn't say anything as he puts down the phone. JOHNNY removes the cap and inhales.

JOHNNY

Wow, so that's what good Scotch smells like. Unfortunately, my street corner don't earn me enough money to buy this kind of stuff. My regular poison costs a little less. But a girl likes to dream. Boy, I bet this would taste great on ice cream.

GEORGE

Would you like a drink?

JOHNNY

Sir, I would really love one or two or maybe a few more. But I better not.

GEORGE

Afraid it will corrupt your palate?

JOHNNY

It's not even ten in the morning. You might want to see somebody about your wanting to drink this early.

GEORGE

I see. I figured someone in your position wouldn't be too particular about the time.

JOHNNY

Actually, a drop of the stuff would kill me, and it's a little early in the day for me to die. Still got a few things to do.

GEORGE

You're not going to die.

JOHNNY

I wish. I know you hated it when we didn't agree with you, but my liver's kinda shot. There's only sawdust left down there. The last time I was in the hospital, the doctor told me one more quickie love affair with the bottle, and I was history. My liver is looking for its own Wounded Knee. And the cavalry is usually 80 proof. So I must be … rude … and refuse your kind hospitality. I'm not ready yet to shuffle off this mortal coil. See, I still remember things from your class. And you said I'd never amount to much.

JOHNNY plops herself down on the couch. She and GEORGE stare at each other for a second or two.

GEORGE

I said that … about you, did I?

JOHNNY

Yep. You said I was kinda smart but didn't apply myself. Lo and behold, I guess you were psychic.

GEORGE

At St. David's?

JOHNNY

Yep. Back in the pre-Scotch days. Pre-wife and family.
Your tastes seemed to have changed over the years.

GEORGE

I resent what you are implying.

JOHNNY

Me, I can't even spell "implying."

Beat.

GEORGE

So?

JOHNNY

So.

GEORGE

Why are you really here?

JOHNNY

Wow. That's a good question. I guess … why are any of
us really here?

GEORGE

I'm here to work. To deliver the word of God. To make the
world a better place.

JOHNNY

Me … I'm a memory. Whose memory, I'm not sure. I know
that I am only half or a quarter of who I used to be. And
somehow, I know that's not right. I was someone once. Or
I was meant to be someone once.

GEORGE

What does that have to do with me?

JOHNNY

I think you know.

GEORGE

Let's pretend I don't.

JOHNNY

Okay, Reverend King –

GEORGE

Assistant Bishop King.

JOHNNY

Forgive me. *Assistant Bishop King*. See, there are parts
of my life I don't remember. Or maybe I do. It gets hard
to tell sometimes. I think I mentioned that. It's like
I'm a ghost, floating through the city, just a shadow of
questionable actions. Sort of like the ghost of abuse past.
There are some things I remember but forget, and the
other way around, too. But some memories are crystal
clear and solid. Things that, as much as I try, as much as
I drink, as much as I cry and bang my head against a brick
wall, won't go away. They're like scars that sit on my
mind, scars that can't be removed no matter what. And
occasionally scars that walk out of Tim Hortons.

GEORGE

Are you trying to blackmail me? With these ... these ...
lies? It won't work.

JOHNNY

No, sir. Not me. What's money to a dead Indian? And I'd
be a little careful with that L-word. Keep in mind who's
looking over your shoulder. I read somewhere your big guy
don't like that.

> *JOHNNY points to the painting, squints at the
> image of Christ.*

GEORGE

St. David's was a very long time ago.

JOHNNY

It was yesterday.

GEORGE

I think we're communicating on two different planes here.
You've obviously had some problems. I understand. I've
done some fieldwork with people who have suffered from
substantial alcohol abuse. It does things to the mind.
I know. You yourself have admitted your memory isn't
what it used to be. That everything is hazy. I think possibly
you're suffering from some sort of delusion. Let me help.
I know a place that –

JOHNNY

No help. I've been helped before. By a lot of white
do-gooders, and a few Indian ones. And trust me,
there's nothing worse than a reformed alcoholic trying
to dry you out. To me, that was even more of a reason
to keep drinking. Those guys are good for a meal and an
occasional warm bed. But have you ever seen those old-
time photographs, where only the centre of the picture
is clear and in focus and everything around it is fuzzy?
That's what I remember. That is what I see in my mind.

GEORGE

That's the thing with delusions, sometimes they can
appear so real –

JOHNNY

Sometimes them delusions *are* real.

GEORGE

And sometimes they're not. Sometimes the mind is
your worst enemy. As I said, I've done some fieldwork
and I know the reality of the streets. Yes, I was there at
St. David's, but I don't remember you, Johnny Indian,

or whatever your name is. And if you are implying
what I think you are implying, your memory is worse
than you say.

JOHNNY

Do you have any Aspirin?

GEORGE

Why?

JOHNNY

I hurt. Why else would somebody want Aspirin?
So, do you?

*GEORGE retrieves a bottle of Aspirin from a desk
drawer and gives JOHNNY two tablets.*

GEORGE

I really think you should go to the hospital – or let me
call a doctor.

JOHNNY

You and your doctors and hospitals and clinics. They
can't cure everything. Or is this just so you can get me
out of here?

GEORGE

I want you to get the help that I can't provide. (*pause*)
Where are you from, Johnny?

JOHNNY

Where am I from … That's a good question.
Where *am* I from?

GEORGE

Do you have a good answer? I mean, St. David's served
an area over three thousand square miles. About a dozen
or more Native communities, if I remember correctly.
Sometimes a few from even farther away. You said

"*noogoom*" earlier. That's means grandmother, doesn't it … in Cree? So that tells me something.

JOHNNY

Ah, you know Cree …

GEORGE

A few words. I've worked with some Cree people over the years and picked up a little bit. It's a beautiful language.

JOHNNY

Sure, *now* it's a beautiful language. Not then. You got any water? These are a bitch to swallow dry.

GEORGE

There's a bottle in my jacket beside you.

> *JOHNNY pulls the bottle of water out of GEORGE's coat and notices something as she does so.*

JOHNNY

Ooh, the fancy stuff. I'm used to water fountains. And can I have two more pills? Not everything makes it through my liver. I have to double up these days.

> *As GEORGE dispenses two more pills, JOHNNY slips his cell phone out of the same pocket as the water and hides it under a cushion. GEORGE hands her the pills.*

JOHNNY

You're a saint.

> *JOHNNY swallows the Aspirin, drinks the rest of the water, then looks at the empty bottle.*

JOHNNY

That's better. Water into wine. Remember that old trick, Assistant Bishop King? There have been a few times I wished I could do that. The best I could do was turn pocket change into cheap sherry.

GEORGE

You didn't answer my question. Where are you from?

JOHNNY

Far, far away. You can't get there from here. At least I can't.

GEORGE

Does this faraway place have a name?

JOHNNY

Home.

GEORGE

A more specific name.

JOHNNY

Again, that would be too easy. I need you to remember me,
by yourself. I don't want to draw you a map. I want you
to find your own way, like I did. But I will give you a hint.
A small, round one. (*pause*) Oranges.

GEORGE

Oranges?! I don't understand. Are you talking about the
oranges we gave you at Christmas?

JOHNNY

You do remember! Oh good. We never could figure out
exactly what oranges had to do with Christ's birthday.
We couldn't find anything in the Bible about oranges in
the manger ... but then, there was a lot we could never
figure out about that place and that story.

GEORGE

I'm sorry. You've lost me. What does that have
to do with you?

JOHNNY

Not with me. With you. There's so much more to those
oranges than Christmas. Or don't you remember?

GEORGE

My memory is fine. I remember all the children being given fruit at Christmas. But that's all. That's all.

JOHNNY

Hmm, I was so sure you'd –

GEORGE tosses JOHNNY her tattered jacket.

GEORGE

Madam, I think it's time for you to go.

JOHNNY

And if I don't want to –

GEORGE

Let's not finish that sentence. Off you go. I've offered to help, but it's obvious –

JOHNNY doubles over in pain and falls to the floor.

JOHNNY

OH JESUS!

GEORGE

What's wrong?!

JOHNNY

I told you. I'm sick. Dying.

GEORGE

What? Here?

JOHNNY

Sometimes Aspirin just doesn't cut it.

GEORGE

I am definitely calling an ambulance.

*GEORGE picks up the phone and begins to dial, but
JOHNNY somehow manages to crawl over and rip
the cord out of the jack.*

GEORGE

Why the hell did you do that?

JOHNNY

I'm not done yet.

GEORGE

I was trying to help you! Look, I've humoured you as much as I can. I am obviously not who you think I am. I will not have you die in my office. I have a cell phone –

*JOHNNY begins to hum a slow melody, "Yesterday"
by the Beatles. GEORGE recognizes it and
stops instantly.*

JOHNNY

(*weakly*) Do you recognize that song, Assistant Bishop King?

GEORGE doesn't react.

JOHNNY

I remember it so good. It's one of those real clear images that's at the centre of the fuzzy photographs in my mind. It wasn't until ten years after I left St. David's that I found out what it's called. "Yesterday" by the Beatles. I was in a shopping mall the first time I'd heard it since I'd left the school. I was sitting by the water fountain when it came over the loudspeakers. Almost immediately my whole body cramped. I was doubled over ... started sweating and ... my stomach was turning inside out. I couldn't breathe. I vomited. And vomited. It's not easy to vomit like that when you got nothing in your stomach. You used to sing us to bed with that song. That was your favourite song. It was the last sound we heard as we fell asleep ... then later that night you would wake us up, for other reasons. I remember. My body remembers.

GEORGE

No, you don't. You just think you do.

JOHNNY

Then I got an awfully good imagination.

GEORGE

My child …

JOHNNY

My child …

GEORGE

It's obvious you've had a great deal of hardship in your
life. I will say a prayer for you. But there's obviously
something wrong here. I am not who you think I am.
There is no possible way I could even contemplate
doing what you are insinuating. It's impossible, I assure
you. Now if –

JOHNNY

Do you know what's really sad? I actually like most of the
Beatles' other stuff. Assistant Bishop King, isn't confession
good for the soul?

GEORGE

You know very well it is. Do you have something you
want to confess? Then confess directly to the Lord. He
is ultimately the only one who can grant absolution.

JOHNNY

Do you think God has forgiven you for what you did?

GEORGE

I will not have this conversation with you. I've done
nothing to be ashamed of. I'm not running. I'm not
hiding. I am standing here looking you in the face,
telling you the truth.

JOHNNY

Yeah, you know, almost like you've been expecting this
to happen. What's it been, Assistant Bishop King, forty
years, thereabouts? Waiting for that knock at the door.
Wondering if somebody will show up and point their
little copper finger at you? A lot of you churchmen aren't
breathing too easy these days, are you, Assistant Bishop
King? I hear about lots of court cases. Lots of apologies.
Lots of ... what are they called ... accusations. A lot of
money being given out. Ever get nervous?

GEORGE

No.

JOHNNY

Not even a little bit?

GEORGE

I have nothing to fear. I am innocent. I sleep well at night.

JOHNNY

Beside your beautiful family.

GEORGE

They and the Church are my life.

JOHNNY

Then I guess you're a lucky man. I had a family ... once.
I had to trade them in for your school. Do you think that
was a fair trade, Assistant Bishop King? My old family
loved me ... I think. I don't know for sure. They, like a lot
of things, were beaten out of me. My past is like a book
with three out of every four pages ripped out. Hints of
what my story was. At that place, I was told Jesus Christ
and God were my new parents. Some parents. Where were
they when I needed them? I guess you could call them
latchkey parents. I'd press charges, but I don't think either
of them would show up in court. It's kind of hard to serve

them papers. The Church, on the other hand, now that's different. They ...

> *GEORGE goes over to the bookshelf and takes*
> *out a book, which he throws on the cushion*
> *beside JOHNNY.*

GEORGE

Do you know what that is?

JOHNNY

I know I've been out of school a while, but ... a book?

GEORGE

A National Crime: The Canadian Government and the Residential School System, 1879–1986. You should read it. It's all about what happened at the residential schools.

JOHNNY

When does the movie come out?

GEORGE

It deals with schools set up by the Catholic, United, and Anglican Churches.

JOHNNY

I knew about the Catholics, but the United, too? They always seem so nice.

GEORGE

I've read that book cover to cover. For years I sat on the committee set up by the Anglican Church to support healing in the communities. I do this because I know what went on.

JOHNNY

I bet you do.

GEORGE

Because I was there. Why do you think I was at

St. David's for only two years? I hated it. It was a travesty of everything we were trying to do. I became a minister to make the world a better place. St. David's was nothing like they told us it would be. We weren't freeing minds or spreading the love of God. We were punishing children for the stupidest of reasons. Making them eat food we wouldn't give a dog. And then lying about what we were doing. St. David's was a four-storey lie shored up in red brick.

JOHNNY

Hey, brother, you're preaching to the converted.

GEORGE

So I left. I had myself transferred out. I had two eyes, two ears. I'm not stupid. The poor food, the substandard education, the hypocrisy, the abuse ... Yes, there was abuse – and not just by the clergy, but by staff and other students. But not by me. I had trouble seeing the point of teaching there. It sickened me.

JOHNNY

So you ran away, while we had to stay behind. Cry me a river, white boy. If you were so innocent and clean, why didn't you tell anybody? Huh?

JOHNNY discovers the pile of food trays. She starts nibbling.

JOHNNY

Mmm, food.

GEORGE

I was young. And naive.

JOHNNY

Naive ... that's "native" without the *t*. I was younger than you. And I lost my ... naiveness ... and my nativeness. (*distracted for a moment by what she's eating*) Hey,

vegetables, I gotta be careful; there might be a vitamin
in here.

GEORGE

   We did what we were told, but that doesn't absolve us. I've
   spent all these years with that sitting on my soul. I should
   have taken some responsibility and … and faced the evil …
   but I couldn't. I didn't know how. I was young. They were
   all my superiors. I was nobody. So I left. I ran away. And
   it's haunted me ever since.

JOHNNY

   You were only following orders, eh? Hey, what kind of
   cheese is this?

GEORGE

   Brie. But I'm not here to be judged by you.

JOHNNY

   And yet, here I am.

GEORGE

   How can you be so sure?

JOHNNY

   That I'm here?

GEORGE

   So sure that I did whatever you believe I did to you?

JOHNNY

   Again, I was there.

GEORGE

   So was I. And I remember it differently. How old were you
   when what you say … happened?

JOHNNY

   You don't remember?

GEORGE

Answer my question. How old were you?

JOHNNY

I had just turned twelve. Somewhere around there.

GEORGE

That was so long ago. You were a kid, in a different environment. You were under such stress. I'm sure all the reverends looked alike. We dressed alike. Talked alike. You could be wrong about me. You *are* wrong. It wasn't me. Upon my faith in the Lord, I have many sins upon my soul, but I am not guilty of that.

JOHNNY

Sorry, but there are some things you just don't forget. Even if another forty years were to pass. Sounds to me like you're the one doing the forgetting. You don't even remember what's so special about the oranges. Maybe you got one of them old-men-losing-their-memory-type diseases. Do you remember a little boy? His name was Sammy. Sammy ... Indian?

GEORGE

Who was he?

JOHNNY

Another student. My best friend. My brother. My late brother.

GEORGE

If I don't remember you, how could I remember him?

JOHNNY

You couldn't. You see, he never existed. At least, that's what the records from St. David's say.

GEORGE

How can I know somebody who never existed?

JOHNNY

Now there's a deep question. 'Cause I remember him,
so well. I remember playing with him in the woods.
Swimming. I remember laughing with him at all his silly
jokes. We used to fish and make forts in the fallen leaves.
He was so trusting. I made him swallow a tadpole once.

GEORGE

I thought you said he didn't exist.

JOHNNY

He doesn't, anymore. We were there for nine months
before he died, and I was only allowed to talk to him
four times. Four times. You see, boys weren't allowed to
play with the girls. I'd see him across the field sometimes.
Sometimes he was so close, but I was always kept away
from my sweet and precious little brother. (*pause*) Why?
Which one of God's laws would be broken by letting
a brother and sister play together?

GEORGE

I can't give you a logical answer. People there just thought
boys and girls together might get into ... mischief. I know
it doesn't make any sense today. I never really understood
it myself, but –

JOHNNY

It don't matter. He died of TB when he turned ten. He
was just one of a bunch of kids who died that year at the
school. But there's no record of him anywhere. Buried
somewhere, forgotten. It's like God reached out and said,
"Nope, nobody named Sammy Indian ever walked this
earth that I made in six days." Him and hundreds of other
kids over the years all gone, with families not ever knowing
what happened to them. They didn't even let me say
goodbye ... How much mischief would that have caused?

GEORGE

You're right, you're right. I'm not sure –

JOHNNY

Tell me, Assistant Bishop King, what do you say to all
those old Indian women with stretch marks that came
from kids that were never born? When my parents came
looking for Sammy later on, there was no record of him
even being sent to the school, or having died at the school.
Sammy ceased to exist. It's like he was a magician. *Poof*,
and he was gone. One less Indian in the world. You guys
tried to tell my mother and father that they had no second
child there at the school. Oddly enough, they had trouble
believing that.

GEORGE

I don't know any of that.

JOHNNY

But if he didn't exist, then where did my memories come
from? Answer me that, Assistant Bishop King. The same
place my memories of you came from?

GEORGE

I don't know anything about your brother. Or about you.
That was more than forty years ago!

JOHNNY

Too bad. Maybe he died before you got to St. David's.
You would have liked him. But maybe he was a little too
young for you. And you liked little girls. Thank heavens for
small mercies, eh?

GEORGE

Will you shut up! I am a man of God. A family man.
A man of respect. I am not a monster.

JOHNNY

I wonder how many like you have said that over the years.
Even the Jesuits thought they were doing something good,
being productive. At least we got to martyr them, eh?

GEORGE pulls a photo album off the shelf and opens it, showing it to JOHNNY.

GEORGE

Look, here I am at the reading of the official apology, in 1993. That's me, in the back row, behind Archbishop Michael Peers. Would I be there if I was guilty?

JOHNNY

You've put on weight.

GEORGE

(reading from the photo album)

"I accept and I confess before God and you, our failures in the residential schools.

"We failed you. We failed ourselves. We failed God.

"I am sorry, more than I can say, that we tried to remake you in our image, taking from you your language and the signs of your identity.

"I am sorry, more than I can say, that in our schools so many were abused physically, sexually, culturally, and emotionally.

"On behalf of the Anglican Church of Canada, I present our apology."

JOHNNY

Pretty words.

GEORGE

Heartfelt words.

JOHNNY

But just words. I could say I love you. I could say I can fly. I could say I'm the second coming of Christ, but we both know those would be just words.

GEORGE

They're not just words. We agonized over what to say. How to say it.

JOHNNY

It reads wonderfully for the news, but I was there. This is about me. (*pause*) I like this picture book of yours. It's like a time machine that shows you climbing your way up the Church's corporate ladder.

GEORGE

If that's how you want to describe it. One of my children put that together for me, two years ago. For my birthday.

JOHNNY

Your family must love you a lot. Do you love them?

GEORGE

What kind of question is that?

JOHNNY

A very important one, I think.

GEORGE

Of course I love them. They are my family.

JOHNNY

What's your wife's name?

GEORGE

I told you, that's not your concern.

JOHNNY picks up the family photograph, turns it over, and reads the back.

JOHNNY

Sarah. And your kids are Ruth, Daniel, and Mary. All good Christian names. (*still reading*) Mary's confirmation. Wow, people still wear white to those things.

GEORGE *forcibly takes the picture from JOHNNY
and puts it back down on the desk.*

GEORGE

Leave them alone.

JOHNNY

Do you want to know why I'm really here?

GEORGE

You've made that painfully obvious, though you are
profoundly misdirected.

JOHNNY

That depends on if you believe in God or not. God must
have sent me.

GEORGE

God? Sent you? And just why would God have
sent you here?

JOHNNY

It's amazingly obvious. He must have wanted me to come
here. Why else would those punks have kicked me off my
corner? Why would I have ended up at Tim Hortons? Why
would you go to that same Tim Hortons? When I was
there too? Don't you see … Tim Hortons must be part of
his master plan!

GEORGE

We had a small party last night and I offered to clean up.
I needed a coffee beforehand, so –

JOHNNY

What kind of party?

GEORGE

To celebrate my promotion to assistant bishop. Some of
the staff thought –

JOHNNY

Well, congratulations, Assistant Bishop King! I didn't
realize it happened so recently. So why would God arrange
for you to be promoted at this very time? Holy mackerel,
it must be some kind of miracle!

GEORGE

It is not a miracle. God has nothing to do with this.
He doesn't send people to Tim Hortons out of some
divine purpose.

JOHNNY

Pretty odd words for an assistant bishop. I thought God
was in all things and all places?

GEORGE

Yes, but if you trip over a rock, I doubt if it's God's fault.
It's your own clumsiness. This ... so-called meeting has all
been a coincidence, I'm sorry to say.

JOHNNY

Coincidence? I thought good Christians didn't believe
in coincidence.

GEORGE

God works in mysterious ways. You may have heard me
say that, too.

JOHNNY

He sure does. Like when he said, "Suffer the little
children," did you guys have to take him so seriously?

GEORGE

Now you're being blasphemous. The passage reads, "And
when Jesus saw it, he was much displeased, and said unto
them, 'Suffer the little children to come unto me, and
forbid them not: for of such is the kingdom of God.'" In
that context, "suffer" means to permit. You're just trying
to pervert his words.

JOHNNY

    Monkey see, monkey do.

GEORGE

    We can't change the past. We can only address it. That's
    why I want to help. You look so tired … exhausted.

JOHNNY

    You're not going to start singing "Yesterday"
    to me, are you?

GEORGE

    I was never fond of that song. Or the Beatles.

JOHNNY

    You guys still upset over that "more popular than Jesus"
    thing? Lennon was probably right. More people know
    "Lady Madonna" than the Sermon on the Mount.

GEORGE

    I think you're thinking of Reverend Anderson.

    JOHNNY's face reveals her confusion.

GEORGE

    He taught music, remember?

JOHNNY

    Reverend …

GEORGE

    … Anderson. Surely you remember him. Tall man. Bald.
    Always smelled of tobacco. Reverend Anderson. He used
    to hum that song all the time.

JOHNNY

    No … no … it was you. I'm …

GEORGE

    I was more into folk music.

JOHNNY

No … it was … you. You.

GEORGE

I'm sorry but, no, it wasn't. You look confused.

JOHNNY

It doesn't matter.

GEORGE

Yes, it does. If you were wrong about that, what else are
you wrong about? I'm not angry, Johnny. Not at all. It's
obvious what has happened to you over the years – how
it's affected you – and it's not your fault.

JOHNNY

It couldn't have been him … *You* hummed it.

GEORGE

Don't you remember how he would sing that song at the
Christmas concert? Usually off-key, but he would try.

JOHNNY

I'm not wrong.

GEORGE

You don't have to get upset. We all make mistakes.

JOHNNY

No, it's not a mistake. I have thought about this for forty
years. It's always there. You're always there.

GEORGE

I hate to say the obvious, but look at how damaged
you are. You can barely even sit up straight. So how can
you trust anything? Could be delirium tremens or any of
a host of other medical problems. You could be delusional,
schizophrenic. All of what you remember about me you
might have dreamed up during some drug or alcohol
binge. It's certainly possible – in fact, it's more than likely.

Your details about me are filtered through many years of
abuse. Memories can lie.

JOHNNY

You're not a detail. You're a ghost, too.

GEORGE

I'm a ghost? How am I a ghost?

JOHNNY

You're a ghost. I'm a ghost. All these memories of what
happened to me, to Sammy, to all of us. They're like ghosts
seen out of the corner of the eye. No one wants to admit
they're real. You can see through them. You can't prove
them. Nobody believes. They don't exist. My childhood
doesn't exist. It's dead. I'm a ghost.

GEORGE

You poor woman …

> GEORGE *moves in to comfort JOHNNY, who*
> *reacts violently.*

JOHNNY

DON'T TOUCH ME!

GEORGE

It's okay. Everything's okay. Just relax. We're all fine here.
Tell me some more, like why are you a ghost, Johnny.

JOHNNY

When my brother died, and my parents came to get us
for the summer, they found out … and I died to them,
too. I was supposed to look after him. But I couldn't do
anything about him being sick. Nobody told me. I didn't
know he'd died for a week, until one of you guys got
around to telling me. Even though they kept Sammy and
me apart, my parents blamed me for not looking after
him. They didn't understand, so I became just as dead to

them as he was. That's why I am a ghost. Those buildings
created a lot of ghosts.

GEORGE
That's … that's horrible.

JOHNNY
Yeah, isn't it?

> *JOHNNY starts to breathe hard and fast. She slumps
> to the ground.*

GEORGE
Here, let me help you.

JOHNNY
Okay. I would greatly appreciate it if you would confess.
Pretty please?

GEORGE
You want me to confess? Fine, I will confess. I confess
I spent two years at St. David's. I confess I heard about
things that happened there, and other places. Horrible
things. I confess I didn't do anything to stop it, as I should
have. I confess I abandoned a sinking ship. I confess
I should have done something. I confess. I confess I've had
to live with that. I confess St. David's failed and I failed.
But that's all I will confess to, because that's all there it to
confess. The confessional is closed. Are you satisfied?

> *Neither of them says anything.*

GEORGE
Let me get you up off the floor.

JOHNNY
No.

GEORGE
You're being silly.

JOHNNY

No, Sammy was the silly one. So silly …

GEORGE

I don't know anything about Sammy. I'm sorry.

JOHNNY

You don't seem to know much about anything, do you?
(*painfully rises to her feet*) An invisible brother. A ghost
of a childhood. A song you didn't sing. Am I really here?

GEORGE

Yes, you are. So, do you believe me now?

JOHNNY

No. Maybe it was Reverend Anderson who sang
"Yesterday" … I don't know anymore.

GEORGE

He's dead now. Though, I did hear rumours about him at
St. David's. That's why I think …

JOHNNY

Maybe he did. Maybe he was one of the bad guys. But
so were you.

GEORGE

Do you have proof? Other people accusing me? Otherwise,
it's just my word against yours.

JOHNNY

No proof. No other witnesses. Just me.

GEORGE

Allegations like yours have to have some basis in truth –
some evidence. We're not handing out blank cheques or
apologies to whoever walks in the door.

JOHNNY

I told you. I don't want any money. Or an apology.

GEORGE

Then what?

JOHNNY

It's a big word, with a big meaning. Acknowledgement.

GEORGE

Of what? For something that may or may not have happened to you?

JOHNNY

No, I want acknowledgement … that I'm me. Me! I'm Sammy's sister. I am my parents' child. I don't want to be a ghost anymore. I want to exist. To be seen. To be noticed. To be acknowledged by you. And to have you admit what you've done.

GEORGE

I'm afraid I can't do that. And I think it's time to call the police.

JOHNNY

Oh, you can't do that.

GEORGE picks up the telephone.

JOHNNY

It's broke, remember?

GEORGE

Damn it!

JOHNNY

Language, Assistant Bishop King.

GEORGE

(*walking to the door*) Fine, I have a cell phone. I can –

GEORGE goes to his coat and searches inside the pockets, but can't find his phone.

GEORGE
    My cell ... it's gone.

JOHNNY
    I guess God does indeed work in mysterious ways, eh?

GEORGE
    Give me back my cell phone.

JOHNNY
    That would make it a lot more difficult to finish our talk.

GEORGE
    I've been very patient but there is a limit to all things.

JOHNNY
    No more Mr. Nice Guy?

GEORGE
    I'm afraid not.

JOHNNY
    Okay. No more Ms. Nice Girl either.

        *JOHNNY pulls a pistol from deep inside a pocket
        of her discarded jacket. She points it at GEORGE,
        who freezes.*

JOHNNY
    I didn't wanna do this.

GEORGE
    Why are you pointing a gun at me?

JOHNNY
    I want your attention.

GEORGE
    Okay, you've got it.

JOHNNY

Those two years you taught at St. David's, when I was
there, too, did you molest me? Did you touch me?

GEORGE

No.

JOHNNY

Did you stick your cock in my mouth? Did you fuck
me? Yes or no?

Silence for a beat or two.

GEORGE

No!

JOHNNY

That's the wrong answer.

GEORGE

It's the only answer. You don't want to kill me, Johnny.
It wouldn't solve anything. It would only make
your life worse.

JOHNNY

I live on the streets, eat garbage, beg to survive, have
nightmares – and I'm dying. How much worse could
it possibly get?

GEORGE

Put the gun down.

JOHNNY

When I'm done with it.

GEORGE

I'm not afraid to die. Why do you want to do this?

JOHNNY

To end this. Make it stop.

GEORGE

Closure? You want closure? I'm sorry, but violence seldom brings closure. It frequently just complicates the situation even more.

JOHNNY

Assistant Bishop King.

GEORGE

We're adults now. You can call me George.

JOHNNY

No thanks.

GEORGE

Do you seriously want to pull that trigger and shoot me?

JOHNNY

No.

GEORGE

Then put the gun down. If you do, I will erase this whole thing from my memory and you can go on your way. No harm done.

JOHNNY

"No harm done." You have a bad habit of picking the wrong phrases. Actually you had a lot of bad habits. Oh, I know you tried to save the child by killing the Indian, but I think some of it managed to hide out somewhere, maybe behind my brown eyes, under my black hair, or beneath my thick skin. Killing an entire people can take a lot of time. I guess ten years wasn't long enough.

GEORGE

Think about this, Johnny.

JOHNNY

I have and I'm conflicted. Isn't that funny?

JOHNNY laughs a hearty laugh. GEORGE doesn't.

GEORGE

It isn't funny. Murder ... revenge isn't funny.

JOHNNY

You sent a six-year-old to jail. For ten years of hard labour, and worse. Forty years of probation ... I've had a long time to think about this moment ... about you.

GEORGE

Johnny, please put down the gun.

JOHNNY holds the gun up to her head.

JOHNNY

I could just shoot myself ... that would solve the problem just as easy. No more tears. No more anything.

GEORGE

Both would damn you.

JOHNNY

I don't think I'd notice the difference. What to do ... What to do ...

Lights go down.

END OF ACT ONE

ACT TWO

GEORGE and JOHNNY are in the same positions as before; they hold them for a few moments.

GEORGE
Well?

JOHNNY
Well what?

GEORGE
For a moment I thought ...

JOHNNY takes the gun away from her head.

JOHNNY
Just seeing if you were paying attention. God, sometimes you white people ain't got no sense of humour. Got any more of that brie?

GEORGE
Oh, Johnny, you play dangerous games.

JOHNNY
A girl's gotta have some fun, don't she?

JOHNNY walks over to the box of bottles, examines the Scotch. She sets the gun down on the coffee table. GEORGE watches her, still hopped up on adrenaline. He steps forward and JOHNNY immediately grabs the gun.

JOHNNY
I hope you're not planning to go anywhere.

GEORGE

I go where I'm needed.

JOHNNY

You're needed here.

GEORGE

Just stretching my legs. I'm not a young man anymore.
They do tend to get a bit stiff.

JOHNNY

I know stiff. We're good buddies. Assistant Bishop King,
have you ever drank Lysol?

GEORGE

Can't say that I have.

JOHNNY

The first drink's the toughest. It burns. But after that,
either the mind or the body blocks it out. Nice buzz
though. And your breath smells pine fresh. We Native
people like that; reminds us of the outdoors.

GEORGE

Am I supposed to laugh?

JOHNNY

You can do whatever you want. You always did.

> JOHNNY *holds up the Scotch, the gun in*
> *her other hand.*

JOHNNY

Bet this costs more than Lysol, don't it?

GEORGE

Substantially.

JOHNNY

Substantially ... I gotta say, I am kinda curious 'bout what
it tastes like.

GEORGE

Curiosity killed the cat.

JOHNNY

Not my clan. Are you really that concerned about my liver?

GEORGE

I am worried about every part of you.

JOHNNY

I bet you are. Why? Because it's your job?

GEORGE

Partially because of that. Partially because we may be to blame for what happened to you. Partially because I like to think it's the right thing to do and that I'm a nice guy.

JOHNNY

You are your brother's keeper.

GEORGE

Exactly.

JOHNNY

I tried doing that once. Like I said, it didn't turn out so well. Oh well, no use crying over buried brothers.

GEORGE

I can only imagine your grief. Let me help. Let us help. We have so many programs –

JOHNNY

(*raising her voice*) Oh god, if I go to one more life-skills class or one more AA meeting, I will shoot myself. If you're so eager to do something good, remember me. Remember Sammy. Remember everything. Take responsibility!

GEORGE

(*yelling*) But you're indicting me without any proof!

JOHNNY

But I remember you. I remember your smell. I remember
your voice. I remember the pain. I remember it all.
All the drinking in the world can't ever get rid of
that. I remember.

GEORGE

You think you do!

> *Their shouting match halts for a moment as they regroup.*
> *JOHNNY's attention turns again to the photograph of*
> *GEORGE's family. She motions to it with the gun.*

JOHNNY

Do *they* know what you did?

GEORGE

Johnny. I don't want to talk about my family. They're not
a part of this.

JOHNNY

Okay, let's talk about mine. I almost had a family once.
A brand new one. One of my own. About ten years or
so after getting out of St. David's, I met a man. He was
very nice, and I really liked him. We had a lot in common.
He'd been to a residential school, too – a different one
though. But he was just as fucked-up as I was. Birds of
a feather, you know.

GEORGE

Do you want me to call him?

JOHNNY

He was Cree, from way up north. A reserve with one of
those long unpronounceable names. His name was Dick.
We met in an upgrading class. I was thinking of going
to college or something. I was trying to become smarter.
God, was I stupid. You guys at St. David's did fuck all
education-wise.

GEORGE

Where is Dick?

JOHNNY

I don't know. I lost him.

GEORGE

He died?

JOHNNY

No, I literally lost him. In a park. It was the weekend and
we'd been on one hell of a bender. Came to early Monday
morning, still time to get home and clean up before class,
but no Dick. He was gone. I waited and waited, even called
a few hospitals and jails, but nothing. He just disappeared.
I guess he fucked off. That happens a lot in my life. Dick –

GEORGE

You said you had a family?

JOHNNY

You see, by then, I wasn't having my moon time ... my
period, as you white people call it.

GEORGE

You were pregnant?!

JOHNNY

Yeah, that happens with Dicks, I hear. But you don't
wanna hear all this woman stuff. It'll just make you ... sad.

GEORGE

It looks like it's making you sad.

JOHNNY

You know, I've never understood why the Church hates
kids. I mean really hate them. No laughing, no playing,
no talking, no love, no nothing. It was like we were being
punished for being kids. Funny, eh?

GEORGE

You were mentioning something about you being
pregnant … did you have a boy or a girl?

JOHNNY

(*working up strength*) A girl. Six pounds, nine ounces
of the cutest little Cree girl you could imagine. Pure
concentrated beauty. She looked so much like Sammy …
so much. I thought I'd actually found something I could
do pretty good. And I thought I could stop being a ghost,
'cause ghosts don't have kids, right? When I was pregnant,
I stopped drinking … mostly, but –

She looks at GEORGE.

JOHNNY

I think you know how this ends, don't you?

GEORGE

I have my fears.

JOHNNY

Seems I was wrong. I couldn't even do that right. The
damage had been done. They called it fetal alcohol
syndrome. I told you you didn't want to hear about this.

GEORGE

I'm so sorry.

JOHNNY

As you can tell, I'm not exactly great mother material.
They took her away from me. Angela. My little angel.
That's what I called her. I don't know what she's called
today, but she was my little angel. At that moment, for the
first time in a very long time, I actually believed in God,
'cause only God could make something so beautiful. Not
somebody like me.

Silence.

GEORGE

It might be possible to find her. There are ways –

JOHNNY

And what possible good would that do? She was better off where she went. Couldn't have raised a kid on day-old doughnuts and handouts from the soup kitchen. Geez, she'd be ... in her twenties by now. Wow. But ghosts can't have children. (*She pauses, weary.*) Like Sammy, it's like she never existed.

GEORGE

Johnny, I'm so sorry.

JOHNNY

So sorry. Afterwards, I was told, no more kids for me. Something got busted up in the process and they took some parts out. The moon never rose for me again. So, I started calling myself by a man's name. Might as well.

GEORGE

Johnny ...

JOHNNY

That's me. I don't even have a picture of her ... not like this one. (*pause*) What are their names?

GEORGE

You know their names. Can I ask you a question, Johnny?

JOHNNY

Sure.

GEORGE

Something you just said, do you believe in God?

JOHNNY

I think the more important question is, does he believe in me?

GEORGE

I think you know the answer to that. I mean, sitting here, listening to you, you sound so very lost.

JOHNNY

So very lost ...

GEORGE

And while you have no reason to trust us, you should trust God. Men will lead you into the darkness, but his light shall lead you out.

JOHNNY

Hallelujah! I might have believed that once. You know, every once in a while I would go through moments of being sober. I would get a job, keep it for a couple months or even a few years. Then the nightmares would start ... Anyways, during those times, I would try to lead a normal life. Hold down a job, pay taxes, ride the bus, ignore street people, feel guilty about my daughter – all the normal middle-class stuff. And it would work. Really. If you were to have seen me then, you wouldn't have recognized me. I had almost become what you and St. David's wanted me to be.

GEORGE

I guess the next thing to do is make those periods of stability last longer. Make your goals attainable.

JOHNNY

There are things I can remember, bits and pieces of stuff from the past forty years. I completely missed the disco years, but I managed to follow the rise of Shania Twain and the two middle years of *North of 60*.

GEORGE

Well, that's something, I suppose. Except for the gun, I'm finding you to be a lucid and intelligent – if misguided – woman. Johnny, you can have a future. It's not too late.

JOHNNY

You mean get a job? Settle down? Would you let a woman like me marry your son?

GEORGE

Johnny, Daniel is eighteen.

JOHNNY

Oh, how about your daughters?

GEORGE

Humour is an excellent sign of healing. So, Johnny, what …

JOHNNY

You had them kind of late in life, eh? Your kids. You must have been in your forties or something.

GEORGE

I didn't marry my wife till I was thirty-nine.

JOHNNY

Why?

GEORGE

I didn't meet her until I was thirty-five.

JOHNNY

I thought you religious people got married early in life. That "go forth and multiply" kind of thing.

GEORGE

Everybody is different.

JOHNNY

Was she older than I was when we met?

GEORGE

Of course. Substantially.

JOHNNY

There's that word again, "substantially." But good for
you. You're adaptable. No more little Indian girls running
around, so you had to make do with older white ones?

GEORGE

The filth that comes from your mouth.

JOHNNY

I only know what I see.

GEORGE

I am not a monster.

JOHNNY

So you keep saying.

GEORGE

I'm not. I can't even contemplate …

JOHNNY

Did your kids have nightmares, Assistant Bishop King,
like me? Did you sing to them …

*GEORGE lunges at JOHNNY, grabbing her
arm forcefully.*

GEORGE

You will not say such disgusting things about my
children, you –

*But JOHNNY still has the gun in her other hand and
she waves it at GEORGE, who backs down.*

JOHNNY

No, no, no, no. I have my get-out-of-jail-free card.

GEORGE

I told you. Leave my family out of this.

JOHNNY

I suppose you left your little girls alone. It's not often
a bird will shit in its own nest. That's an old Indian saying
or something.

GEORGE

I would have died before I let anything happen
to my children.

JOHNNY

Children are so important. It's good you finally learned
that. Better late than never, eh? "For I, the Lord, thy God,
am a jealous god, visiting the iniquity of the fathers upon
the children unto the third and fourth generations." That's
your great-great-grandkids, Assistant Bishop King. That's
a long time for your family to suffer because of your
"iniquities." "Train up a child in the way he should go:
and when he is old, he will not depart from it." Remember
that? Basic residential school logic. The one who is hurt
becomes the hurter. I'm glad my little Angela is with
a good family far away from me, for that would be the last
straw. I know the pain will end with me. Assistant Bishop
King, I've got a question. Think you can answer it for me?

GEORGE

What?

JOHNNY

Catholic priests aren't allowed to marry or have sex. So,
they got all these built-up, frustrated urges bouncing off
the church walls. They got to do something with them,
so they grab the nearest little girl, or boy, to get it out of
their system. Maybe that's what's causing all their abuse
problems, eh? I've heard people say that. But Anglican
ministers, you guys can marry. You can fool around.
You can even squeeze a boob without going to hell.
And yet you still find the need to repeatedly diddle kids.
Explain that to me?

GEORGE

I would if I could. I would if I were able. I would if I were responsible. But for the last time, you have the wrong man. At some point you're going to have to understand that and accept it.

JOHNNY

Turn the other cheek?

GEORGE

No. I agree that evil should be punished. Every man in this world has his own demons to fight. Some far worse than others. Why do people hurt children … I don't know. It's beyond me. Is it the Devil at work … I think people blame the Devil for too much and are afraid to take responsibility for their own actions.

JOHNNY

God made man in his own image. Does that make God a child diddler, then?

GEORGE

It's called free choice. Man makes his own choices. That was his greatest gift to us. And greatest curse.

JOHNNY

It depends on who has the free will. I certainly didn't. None of the kids at St. David's did. We couldn't do a damn thing. I don't think God likes Indians.

GEORGE

You are accusing God of being racist now.

JOHNNY

"In the beginning there was darkness, and God said, 'Let there be white.' And there was. And it was good."

GEORGE

He said, "Let there be *light*."

JOHNNY

Light. White. Right. Fright. Not much difference. And do
you know what I find really funny? When good church
people are faced with big, serious decisions in their lives,
they say, "What would Jesus do?" I hope you weren't
thinking that when you came for those evening visits all
those years ago, Assistant Bishop King.

GEORGE

You will say anything, won't you? No matter
how repulsive.

JOHNNY

Like I keep saying, I only know what I was told or shown.
If you damn me, sir, you will damn me only for that. Then
the fault is yours and St. David's.

GEORGE

You are blameless, then?

JOHNNY

No, sir. I am to blame for a lot of things. Too many things.
Just ask whoever took care of Angela. I loved her with
every part of me possible, and it wasn't enough. I had
hurt her before I even knew she existed. And I go to bed
knowing that every night. You see, I think hell is knowing
everything you are responsible for. Blame … I have done
a lot of things that I shouldn't have. I broke the law. Lied
every which way possible. Sold myself. Stole. Hurt people.
Practically everything the Ten Commandments told me
not to do. It's not easy for a woman to stay alive on the
streets. But us Native people, we have a really strong will
to survive. You see, I think it comes down to the fact that
the Church's will to destroy us was never as strong as our
will to live. (*pause*) If you call this living.

GEORGE

Do you know they shut down St. David's? It's now
just a ruin, a shell of a place. Maybe you should make

a pilgrimage there. It might help you heal. Get rid of some of those –

JOHNNY

No. I don't think that would help.

GEORGE

You never know. It might.

JOHNNY

I think you've got the wrong idea. The school itself don't matter. It's just a brick building, a spiritless place that couldn't care less about Johnny Indian or Sammy Indian or anybody else. The Church don't have hands that touch you. It don't come to your room and hurt you. It don't lock doors. It don't sing songs. It don't make kids cry. But *people* – like you and other "servants of God" – are different. They have hands. They have tongues. They have cocks. They have needs. A building can't touch a kid. The people who work there can make kids cry. The Church was the gun, but you were the bullets.

They stare at each other as her words sink in.

GEORGE

I … I don't know how to respond to that …

Suddenly, JOHNNY once again seems wracked with pain. Moving away from GEORGE, she tries to make herself comfortable. GEORGE watches her closely.

JOHNNY

Shit, some of that free will sure comes back to haunt you.

GEORGE

You seem to be getting worse. Johnny, what are you going to do with me? At some point you are going to have to make a choice.

JOHNNY

What am I going to do with you? That is a good question.
I don't know.

GEORGE

That's some master plan you have there.

JOHNNY

I got a short attention span. Every morning I wake up.
That in itself is a good beginning. And then I'm just
happy to make it through to nighttime. Usually that's
a good day for me.

GEORGE

The gun. Where did you get the gun?

JOHNNY

I know. It's very American, isn't it? I found it. In the park.
The same park where I lost Dick. Only I found this a lot
more recently. The Lord did indeed provide, though I don't
really think it's a fair trade.

GEORGE

That gun could have been used in a crime or something.
You should turn it in to the police.

JOHNNY

One way or another, I'm sure it will find its way to the
police. But I'm not done with it yet.

GEORGE

Do you even know how to use that thing?

JOHNNY

I remember my father going hunting. I'd watch him
clean his gun after every trip. He let me shoot it once.
Me, a five-year-old girl. Just about took my shoulder off.
My mother chewed him out for that. Oh, was she angry.
He just laughed.

GEORGE

Those were probably hunting rifles. That's a handgun.
A very different weapon.

JOHNNY

I haven't remembered that in a long time. What do you
know about guns?

GEORGE

Not much. But, like your father, I do know they need to
be cleaned and oiled regularly. Especially if they've been
left in parks. Dirt and dust can cause them to misfire.
And somehow I don't think you have a gun-cleaning kit.
You might end up doing yourself more damage than me
if you decide to shoot that thing. Is that what you want?
Give me the gun.

JOHNNY

I'll give you the bullet.

GEORGE

Very well. (*pause*) If you have a gun, why didn't you use it
on those punks you said took your panhandling spot?

JOHNNY

I thought about it. Oh, that would have been so much
fun, but there's only one bullet in this gun, and I wasn't
going to waste it on them. I've been saving this bullet for
a very long time.

GEORGE

I see. (*pause*) Well, I'm tired of all this. Do you mind if
I pour myself a drink?

JOHNNY

If that's what you want.

GEORGE

What I want is to end this. But a drink will have to
do until then.

JOHNNY

Isn't it a little early in the morning for you non-street people?

GEORGE

Right now I have enough adrenaline coursing through my body to do me for the day. A drink might help. (*pours himself a drink*) Are you thirsty? Can I offer you something?

JOHNNY

I smell coffee.

GEORGE

That I can provide. But we don't have any milk ...

JOHNNY

Lots of sugar. My liver can still process all that stuff.

> GEORGE *sweetens the coffee and passes*
> *it to JOHNNY.*

JOHNNY

Mmm, good. It's not Tim Hortons, but it will do.

GEORGE

Look, Johnny, how long are we going to sit here staring at each other, making accusations and small talk? I was only planning to be here for an hour or so. Pretty soon, people will begin to miss me.

JOHNNY

Let's cross that bridge when we get to it, okay?

GEORGE

No. I've let you dictate this whole situation, say the most obscene things, but it's obvious you would be content to stay here all day waiting for me to confess – and it won't happen. The only possible outcome of this involves the police, who have a lot of their own weapons. They do not take kindly to people waving handguns around. I don't want you to be shot, Johnny. There are options.

JOHNNY

What options?

GEORGE

Give it up. The gun. This whole fiasco. Everything. Or kill me.

JOHNNY

Or kill you. Those are pretty limited options.

GEORGE

Those seem to be your only ones.

JOHNNY

Hey, I could shoot you in the crotch. The middle ground. You'd still be alive, but you'd be kinda unable to pitch. How do you feel about that?

GEORGE

Unenthusiastic.

JOHNNY

I could shoot myself. I could still do that.

GEORGE

No, Johnny. That, too, would be an unforgivable sin. Killing yourself is a grave offence, and an irreversible one.

JOHNNY

So, if you don't want me to shoot myself, I take it you'd rather have me shoot you? You religious people are weird.

GEORGE

We try to look at the big picture. With a little help, all things are possible. I know other people who have gone through what you have and who are managing to lead productive, happy lives. They are dealing with it.

JOHNNY

A thousand leaves can fall from the tree and they'll all land on the ground differently. I landed kind of hard.

GEORGE

All right then. Would you really shoot me, Johnny? If push came to shove, would you put a bullet through my head? Would that make the nightmares go away? Would it avenge Sammy and Angela? Would that make Johnny Indian sleep better? Would it?

JOHNNY

It's better than doing nothing. Something is always better than nothing.

GEORGE

I don't think you could do it. Pull the trigger.

JOHNNY

Oh, you do not want to play that game.

GEORGE

I think it is a game. I don't think you're serious. How do I know if you even have a bullet in that thing?

JOHNNY

It's not much use without one. I know that much. But if it is empty, I could always throw it at you. It is kind of heavy.

GEORGE

That's almost funny.

GEORGE drains his drink.

JOHNNY

Finished. Feel better?

GEORGE

A little. How are *you* feeling?

JOHNNY

Pretty good, all things considered. I see that light at the end of the tunnel.

GEORGE

Could be a train coming directly at you.

JOHNNY

Either way, it will be over.

GEORGE

Will it? How?

> JOHNNY *fires a bullet at the family photograph, nearly missing* GEORGE, *who reacts by falling over onto his back. He crawls away like a crab.*

GEORGE

My god, Johnny! Why did you do that?!

JOHNNY

I don't think you believed me. That I would use this. I think you believe me now.

GEORGE

You're crazy!

JOHNNY

No … I think "dissociative" is the term they used to describe me once. Not quite sure what it means.

GEORGE

You … you … said you had only one bullet. You just used your one bullet. Ha!

JOHNNY

I lied. I have two. I think. No, it's three. See, can't remember shit these days, especially numbers. Never was good at math. Care to see if I got any bullets left?

GEORGE

No, no, I don't. But, Johnny, look at you. You're shaking. Sweating. I really wish you'd stop waving that gun around.

JOHNNY

All those years ago … you'd pretend to be nice to me, like you were my friend, then you'd hurt me. All these years you hoped I'd forgotten, but I didn't. It's been so long, you probably almost forgot.

GEORGE

I never hurt you, Johnny.

JOHNNY

Liar.

GEORGE

In my life I have committed many sins, but that is not one of them.

JOHNNY

Yes, you have! Yes, you have! Why won't you admit it? You're just afraid your wife and family will find out. That's it, eh? You don't want them to know. Or your bosses! You're just afraid, aren't you? Aren't you!

GEORGE

I'm not afraid.

JOHNNY

I can wait all day. All day.

GEORGE

You will have to wait a lot longer.

> *JOHNNY gets noticeably weaker. The last outburst seems to have sapped all her energy.*

GEORGE

Though I don't think you can.

JOHNNY

I've waited over forty years. I can wait longer.

GEORGE

Johnny, unless you get some help, I doubt you'll see the
end of the day —

JOHNNY

Stay away. I said that back then and I'm saying that now.

GEORGE

This can't be doing your condition any good. (*pause*) You
know, there is a third way out of this.

JOHNNY

A third way? What third way?

GEORGE

I will be honest with you, Johnny. Yours is not the first
allegation about St. David's.

JOHNNY

I knew it.

GEORGE

Reverend Anderson and Reverend LeBrett were under
suspicion. Some allegations came forward in the late
eighties. But Reverend Anderson died in '76 and Reverend
LeBrett in '91. With them gone, there was little we could
do. But we did try.

JOHNNY

You've been jerking me around. You knew all the time.

GEORGE

This is the first allegation against me. Remember LeBrett?
He was young like me, and had the same kind of hair.
Maybe it was him, Johnny. Maybe it was him.

JOHNNY

I don't believe anything you say.

GEORGE

We could open an internal investigation. As I said, we believe in cleaning up our own messes. We could launch an inquiry. You could testify. What do you think of that?

JOHNNY

You'd just lie. How many of you guys have actually gone to jail for what you've done?

GEORGE

I don't know. (*pause*) So I take it you're not interested in my suggestion?

JOHNNY

The fox would be watching the henhouse.

GEORGE

So it's a stalemate again.

JOHNNY

Help yourself to another drink. Maybe it will loosen your tongue. I remember how loose your tongue used to be.

GEORGE studies JOHNNY for a second and takes a deep breath.

GEORGE

Okay, I've had enough. (*stands up and straightens his clothes*) I'm leaving.

JOHNNY

You move and I will shoot.

GEORGE

Then shoot. Go ahead. I already told you I don't think you have it in you. It's easy to shoot a chair, but not a real person.

> GEORGE *walks to the door. JOHNNY points the gun at him, desperately trying to intimidate the man.*

JOHNNY

I will! I will!

GEORGE

THEN DO IT!

> GEORGE *puts his hand on the doorknob and JOHNNY changes tactics. On the verge of tears, she turns the gun to her own head.*

JOHNNY

You bastard! You fucking bastard! I'm not joking this time!

> GEORGE *stops. It looks like JOHNNY could really do it this time.*

GEORGE

Johnny, take it easy.

JOHNNY

I'll do it! I swear I'll do it!

> GEORGE *backs away from the door. JOHNNY doesn't move.*

GEORGE

There's no need to do this, Johnny. Everything's okay. I'll stay.

JOHNNY

It looks like you were right. I couldn't do it. I wanted to pull the trigger. I tried. I tried really hard. But …

GEORGE

It's okay, Johnny. I'm still here.

JOHNNY

You deserve to die. You all do. But I can't. I'm weak. I'm the one who's dead.

GEORGE

That's not true. Let me help –

JOHNNY

KEEP AWAY!

GEORGE backs away, placating her.

GEORGE

Okay! Okay. I could spend hours standing here trying to explain what happened in those schools, but it wouldn't make a difference. There is no excusing it. We both know that. But if you break something, you have two choices: you can walk away, forget about it, and let other people deal with it; or you can try and fix it.

JOHNNY

How do you fix a people? How are you going to fix me?

GEORGE

A hospital. Some counselling maybe, for a start. Just don't give up, Johnny.

JOHNNY

I won't. At least not yet. Not while we still have some unfinished business.

GEORGE

That business is finished.

JOHNNY

I will say this for you, Assistant Bishop King, you don't rattle easy.

GEORGE and JOHNNY both sit and wait. They are silent, motionless. The tension between them becomes uncomfortable.

GEORGE

This is ridiculous. You have no idea what to
do now, do you?

JOHNNY

Oh, I know what to do. If you try to leave again, I will
shoot. If not you, then me. Either way, you'll have to have
your carpet cleaned.

Another long silence.

GEORGE

So what now, then?

JOHNNY

I'm thinking.

GEORGE

You're some hostage taker. The state you're in, I could just
wait here until you pass out.

JOHNNY

I won't pass out. At least not until I get what I came for.

GEORGE

When you came in here, what exactly did you
expect of me?

JOHNNY

I expected the truth.

GEORGE

You've got it. We're done.

JOHNNY

I expected that if you were truly as religious as you claim,
you couldn't lie. Especially with him looking down on you.

JOHNNY stares intently at the painting of Christ.

JOHNNY
    He looks so kind. If he only knew ...

GEORGE
    He does know.

JOHNNY
    When you see him, what are you going to tell
    him? To his face.

GEORGE
    Everything I've said to you.

JOHNNY
    You'd lie to the boss? Why stop now, eh?

GEORGE
    Johnny ...

JOHNNY
    Assistant Bishop King ...

GEORGE
    What if I did confess?

JOHNNY
    Yeah ...

GEORGE
    Would that stop the nightmares? If I admitted to every-
    thing you claimed I did, would it make you sleep at night?
    Would it make you put down the gun? Would that light at
    the end of the tunnel show you the way? Tell me, Johnny,
    if I said I abused you all those years ago, what would
    happen? What would change?

JOHNNY
    What ...?

GEORGE

Okay. I did it. I was a terrible man. I did terrible things.
I lied. I committed unspeakable sins. I tried not to hurt
you, Johnny, I really did. I remember stroking your hair
afterwards. Indian children always had such beautiful,
shiny black hair. I'm sorry.

*JOHNNY is shocked. She doesn't know
how to respond.*

JOHNNY

You don't believe that. You're just saying it.

GEORGE

Does it matter?

JOHNNY

Yes, it matters. Of course it matters. I don't want you to
say it just to say it. I want to see the same pain in you that
I see every day in myself. Don't lie to me, you bastard!

GEORGE

So, let me get this straight. You won't accept a denial and
you won't accept a confession? I seem to be damned if I do
and damned if I don't. What to do?

JOHNNY

I'll tell you what to do! Make me believe. Make Sammy
believe you. Make Angela believe you.

GEORGE

I've tried. You won't believe anything I say or do. Kind of
puts me in a difficult position.

JOHNNY

This is important to me. This is all I have.
Don't play games!

GEORGE

That's what we've been doing all morning. I'm just calling
it what it is. Here, let's play another game.

GEORGE uncorks one of the bottles.

JOHNNY

What are you doing?

GEORGE

Starting a new game. You seem to want to play. I want you
to smell this.

He hands JOHNNY the bottle. She is confused.

GEORGE

What does it smell like?

JOHNNY

(*inhales*) It's ... oranges!

GEORGE

Grand Marnier. It's a liqueur made from oranges. Quite
tasty. Now, if I remember correctly, you mentioned
something earlier about oranges, didn't you?

JOHNNY

You used them to bribe us.

GEORGE

I used oranges to bribe you.

JOHNNY won't let go of the bottle.

JOHNNY

I'd never had oranges before. They were so sweet and juicy.
I remember them. That was so long ago. I haven't had an
orange since. Bad memories, the things you made us do.
Can't stand them now.

GEORGE

Johnny, you don't seem to be enjoying this game. Would you like to play something else?

JOHNNY

I once kissed Dick after he'd just eaten an orange. I almost threw up.

GEORGE

They can make liqueur out of just about everything. I once was given a bottle of something made from maple syrup, of all things. Very Canadian, I thought. Didn't taste like maple syrup at all. More like bad Scotch. This, however, still retains the flavour of oranges, don't you think?

JOHNNY

(*in tears*) I hate you.

GEORGE

Are you ready to put down the gun now?

> *JOHNNY weakens. Her resolve evaporates. She looks at the gun in her hand and sets it down on the desk.*

GEORGE

That's a good girl. So, Johnny, it's been quite the exciting morning, eh? I guess that is something I should also apologize for. I believe what you say, Johnny, I really do. But it wasn't me. So now what should we do?

> *JOHNNY is silent.*

GEORGE

So now you're quiet after chewing my ear off all morning.

> *GEORGE picks up the gun and examines it before tucking it in a drawer.*

GEORGE

My goodness, this thing does have another bullet in it.
I guess I owe you another apology for doubting you.

JOHNNY

It's over.

GEORGE

Yes, it is.

JOHNNY

You do owe me an apology. A real one. For Sammy. For
Dick. For Angela. For me. It's got to end.

GEORGE

Oh for ... let's not start that again, Johnny. Let's see what
we can do about you now.

JOHNNY

You win. I can't make you confess. It's that free-will
thing of yours.

GEORGE

It's not exactly mine. I will –

JOHNNY

I was no different with the gun. I forced you to confess.

GEORGE

But I have the gun now, so everything is all right. You're
going to be okay. Now, to –

JOHNNY

I'm tired. I'm sick. I'm through with you. I don't need your
confession anymore. I have all I need up here. (*points to
her head*) It's all here. If you want to hide behind what you
think you believe, then go ahead. I know the truth ...

GEORGE

No, you don't. You just think you do.

JOHNNY

I'm going to leave now.

GEORGE

I don't think that's in your best interests, Johnny. You need help. Everything that's just happened proves it.

JOHNNY

Would you shoot me if I tried to leave?

GEORGE

Of course not.

JOHNNY

That's good to know.

GEORGE

Where will you go?

JOHNNY

Somewhere. There's nothing for me here.

GEORGE

I don't believe there's anything for you out there.

JOHNNY

Nothing out there ever hurt me as much as what's in here. I'll survive.

She puts on her jacket.

GEORGE

You're just going to wander the streets?

JOHNNY

For a while. And what will you do, Assistant Bishop King, once I walk out this door?

GEORGE

Maybe I'll follow you until you can't walk anymore. Then I'll get you to a hospital.

JOHNNY

I don't think you should. You might not like what you see.

GEORGE

I just can't let you walk out of here ... the way you are.
It wouldn't be right.

JOHNNY

It's a little late to be talkin' about what's right and wrong,
isn't it? (*sees the Bible on his desk*) You know, one thing
I could never figure out. I don't remember anywhere in this
thing it saying that Jesus ever laughed. Why is that?

GEORGE

It does say he wept. Wept for the children.

JOHNNY

I guess we know why, eh? I was taught that when God
discovered he was alone, he created laughter. When man
discovered he was alone, he created tears. My granny told
me that once, a long time ago. Maybe. Who remembers ...

GEORGE

That ... Johnny, I remember somebody telling me that,
too. A long time ago. I thought it was so beautiful.
A young girl ... her name was ... what was it ... Lucy?

Laughing painfully, JOHNNY opens the door.

JOHNNY

Very good. It's always nice to be remembered. I was named
after my grandmother ... an old woman in big, baggy
skirts. That's what I remember. She smiled a lot. But she
had more to smile about. And you, King David, I will leave
you with whatever you hold important. But I know that
you've lied. To me. To your family. To God. To yourself.
That's gotta suck.

GEORGE

No, it doesn't. An impaired memory is not something
I will feel guilty about.

JOHNNY

I could have killed you, you know, like I thought I was
going to. *Bang*, and you would have been gone. But
I didn't. That surprised even me. I guess in the end it
wouldn't have really solved anything. Wanting and doing
are two different things. Goodbye, Assistant Bishop King,
I've got places to do, things to go …

GEORGE

Ka … Ka … Ka-wapamitin … Lucy.

JOHNNY

(*laughs*) No. No goodbyes. No Lucy. Johnny. Lucy's
dead. She's been dead for a very long time. I'm a ghost,
remember? (*pause*) Boo.

> She exits through the door. GEORGE begins to
> follow her, then changes his mind. Sitting down at
> his desk, he attempts to drink from his empty Scotch
> glass. Taking a deep breath, he opens the drawer to
> retrieve the gun, but mysteriously it's not there. He
> checks another drawer. The gun is gone. Puzzled, he
> turns toward the picture of Jesus and the children
> as the sound of children's voices and the hymn echo
> in his memory.
>
> Lights go down.
>
> END

Ojibway writer Drew Hayden Taylor lives on the Curve Lake Reserve in Ontario. Hailed by the Montreal *Gazette* as one of Canada's leading Native dramatists, he writes for the screen as well as the stage and contributes regularly to North American Native periodicals and national newspapers. His plays have garnered many prestigious awards, and his beguiling and perceptive storytelling style has enthralled audiences in North America, Europe, and Australia.

Among Taylor's many awards are the Canada Council Victor Martyn Lynch-Staunton Award for Theatre (2009); the Governor General's Award for Drama (nominee, 2006, for *In a World Created by a Drunken God*); the Siminovitch Prize in Theatre (nominee, 2005); James Buller Aboriginal Theatre Award for Playwright of the Year (1997, for *Only Drunks and Children Tell the Truth*); and the Dora Mavor Moore Award for Outstanding New Play, Small Theatre Division (1996, for *Only Drunks and Children Tell the Truth*).